The Best 50
FUDGE RECIPES

Marcia

NITTY GRITTY
Lanham • New York • Boulde

NITTY GRITTY COOKBOOKS
4501 Forbes Boulevard, Suite 200, Lanham, Maryland 20706
www.rowman.com
10 Thornbury Road, Plymouth PL6 7PP, United Kingdom
Distributed by National Book Network

© 2004 Bristol Publishing Enterprises

ISBN: 978-1-55867-290-1 (pbk : alk. paper)

Cover design: Frank J. Paredes
Illustration: Caryn Leschen
Cover Photo: © Foodpix/Shimon & Tammar

♾™ The paper used in this publication meets the minimum requirements of American National
Standard for Information Sciences—Permanence of Paper for Printed Library Materials,
ANSI/NISO Z39.48-1992. Printed in the United States of America

SIMPLE TIPS FOR GREAT FUDGE

Candy making is an art, but it's one you can master with ease. And fudge is a great place to start. A few tips will help you produce great fudge.

You'll need a large, heavy saucepan for boiling the syrup: heavy so the sugar won't burn; and large so that it won't boil over. You may wish to butter the insides of your saucepan, which will help keep sugar crystals from forming. A damp pastry brush also can solve this problem; periodically wash down the sides of the pan while the syrup is boiling.

A candy thermometer is a helpful tool, and simple to use. Make sure that the bulb of the thermometer doesn't touch the bottom of the pan, or you'll get an inaccurate reading. If you're boiling your syrup in the microwave, test the temperature after you've removed the bowl from the microwave, or use a special microwave-safe thermometer.

If you don't have a candy thermometer, you can use the same method as your grandmother did for testing the syrup. Have a glass of very cold (no ice) water nearby. Drop a tiny amount (half a teaspoon or so will do) of the hot syrup into the cold water, and remove it. If you can form a soft ball with the cooled syrup that flattens a bit when you put it down, that's the soft ball stage, or about 238°. If the ball is firm and only slightly pliable, you've reached the hard ball stage, or about 248°.

When making fudge containing cream, butter, milk or chocolate, boil them slowly over fairly low heat until the correct temperature or stage is reached for your recipe. Usually, this mixture will then be set off the heat to cool. You may add butter or flavorings at this point, but just pour it on top of the cooling candy; don't stir until the syrup has cooled to room temperature. Then you can beat in your remaining ingredients and they'll incorporate beautifully. Beat until the fudge is really creamy and smooth.

It's a good idea to line your pans with foil or waxed paper, letting a few inches hang over the sides of the pan. Then when your fudge is cool, you can simply lift it out of the pan and cut it into squares—much easier than trying to cut in the pan. If you score your fudge in the pan while it's slightly warm, it'll make cutting easier. Resist the temptation to cut cooked fudge until it's cooled, or it will lose its shape. Store fudge in the refrigerator or in an airtight container in a cool, dry place.

BUTTERSCOTCH FUDGE

Makes about 36 pieces

The orange zest adds zing to the creamy butterscotch.

1 cup chopped walnuts, divided
1 jar (7 oz.) marshmallow crème
1½ cups sugar
1 can (6 oz.) evaporated milk
4 tbs. (½ stick) butter
¼ tsp. salt
1 pkg. (12 oz.) butterscotch chips
1 tsp. orange extract
1 tsp. grated orange zest

Line an 8-inch square pan with foil. Spread half the walnuts in the pan. In a heavy saucepan over medium heat, combine marshmallow crème, sugar, milk, butter and salt. Bring to a rolling boil, stirring constantly. Boil for 5 minutes, stirring constantly. Remove from heat. Add butterscotch chips. Stir until melted. Stir in extract and zest. Pour into prepared pan. Sprinkle remaining nuts on top. Refrigerate until firm.

For vanilla nut fudge: Substitute 6 oz. white chocolate, chopped, for the butterscotch chips.

CHOCOLATE COCONUT FUDGE

Makes about 36 pieces

For an exotic twist, try toasting the coconut and using dark chocolate instead of milk chocolate.

1 jar (7 oz.) marshmallow crème
1½ cups sugar
1 can (6 oz.) evaporated milk
4 tbs. (½ stick) butter
¼ tsp. salt

1 pkg. (6 oz.) milk chocolate chips
1 cup shredded coconut, divided
1 tsp. orange extract
1 tsp. grated orange zest

Line an 8-inch square pan with foil. In a heavy saucepan over medium heat, combine marshmallow crème, sugar, milk, butter and salt. Bring to a rolling boil, stirring constantly. Boil for 5 minutes, stirring constantly. Remove from heat. Add chocolate chips. Stir until melted and mixture is smooth. Stir in ¾ cup of the coconut, orange extract and orange zest. Pour into prepared pan. Sprinkle remaining coconut on top, pressing gently into surface. Refrigerate until firm.

MARSHMALLOW CRÈME FUDGE

Makes about 36 pieces

Use any type of nuts you like, from peanuts to exotic macadamias.

1 jar (7 oz.) marshmallow crème
1 1/2 cups sugar
1 can (6 oz.) evaporated milk
3/4 cup (1 1/2 sticks) butter or margarine
3/4 tsp. salt
2 pkg. (6 oz. each) semisweet chocolate chips
1/2 cup chopped nuts
1 tsp. vanilla extract

Line an 8-inch square pan with foil. In a heavy saucepan over medium heat, combine marshmallow crème, sugar, milk, butter and salt. Bring to a rolling boil, stirring constantly. Boil for 5 minutes, stirring constantly. Remove from heat. Add chocolate and stir until melted. Stir in nuts and vanilla. Pour into prepared pan. Refrigerate unti! firm.

CREAMY OLD-FASHIONED FUDGE

Makes about 50 pieces

Remember the fudge Grandma used to make? Here's the recipe.

3 cups sugar
1¼ cups milk
4 oz. unsweetened chocolate
2 tbs. corn syrup

4 tbs. (½ stick) butter or margarine
1 tsp. vanilla extract
1½ cups chopped walnuts, pecans
  or almonds

Line a 9-inch square pan with foil. Combine sugar, milk, chocolate and corn syrup in a 3-quart saucepan. Mix well. Cook over medium heat, stirring constantly, until boiling. Lower heat to medium-low. Wipe sugar crystals that form on side of pan with wet pastry brush. Boil until mixture reaches 238° on a candy thermometer or until a small amount of syrup dropped into cold water can be formed into a soft ball. Remove from heat and add butter. DO NOT STIR. Cool to lukewarm. Add vanilla and beat until candy thickens and begins to lose its gloss. Quickly stir in nuts and spread in prepared pan. Refrigerate until firm.

CHOCOLATE-DRIZZLED FUDGE

Makes about 60 pieces

So good, it won't taste like you made it in the microwave!

1¹/₂ cups sugar
1 can (5 oz.) evaporated milk
¹/₄ cup butter or margarine
1 jar (7 oz.) marshmallow crème

1 cup chunky peanut butter
1 tsp. vanilla extract
2 oz. semisweet chocolate

Line an 8- or 9-inch square pan with foil. Place sugar, milk and butter in a microwave-safe 3-quart dish with straight sides. Microwave on high for 6 minutes, stirring after 3 minutes. Microwave on high 4 to 6 minutes longer, until mixture reaches 238° on a candy thermometer. DO NOT place candy thermometer in microwave. Add the marshmallow crème, peanut butter and vanilla; beat until well blended. Pour into prepared pan and smooth top. Refrigerate until firm. Place semisweet chocolate in small glass measuring cup and microwave on high 1 minute, or until just melted. Drizzle the melted chocolate over the fudge.

CANDY STORE FUDGE

Resisting a bite of this creamy fudge would be hard. You'll think you just bought it from a candy shop.

1/2 cup butter, cut into 4 pieces	2 cups sugar
1 pkg. (6 oz.) semisweet chocolate chips	1 can (6 oz.) evaporated milk
	10 large marshmallows
1 tsp. vanilla extract	1 cup chopped nuts

Line an 8-inch square pan with foil. Combine the butter, chocolate and vanilla in a bowl. Set aside. Place the sugar, evaporated milk and marshmallows in a saucepan. Bring to a boil over medium heat. Reduce heat to low and cook, stirring constantly, until the marshmallows have melted and the mixture has thickened a bit, about 6 minutes. Pour the hot mixture over the chocolate mixture in the bowl. Beat with an electric mixer until the fudge is thick and no longer glossy, 4 to 5 minutes. Stir in the nuts. Pour into prepared pan. Refrigerate until firm.

CONFECTIONER'S SUGAR FUDGE

Makes about 64 pieces

This is so tempting, few people can resist it.

2 lb. confectioner's sugar
2 cans (6 oz. each) evaporated milk
2 tbs. butter
2 pkg. (6 oz. each) semisweet chocolate chips
6 tbs. marshmallow crème
1 cup chopped nuts

Line an 8-inch square pan with foil. Combine sugar, milk and butter in a heavy saucepan. Bring to a boil, stirring constantly. Boil 4 minutes. Remove from heat and add chocolate chips and marshmallow crème. Beat until chocolate melts and fudge thickens. Add chopped nuts. Pour into prepared pan. Refrigerate until firm.

MOLASSES FUDGE

Makes about 36 pieces

Angelica, which you can find in the baking aisle, is actually an herb whose stalks are candied. It adds chewy contrast to the creamy fudge.

1 cup brown sugar, packed
1 cup sugar
3 tbs. molasses
1/2 cup heavy cream
1/4 cup (1/2 stick) butter, melted

1 1/2 tsp. orange extract
1/4 cup chopped angelica
2 squares (1 oz. each) unsweetened
    chocolate, chopped

Line an 8-inch square pan with foil. Combine the sugars, molasses, cream and butter in a saucepan over medium heat. Bring to a boil and boil for 3 minutes, stirring quickly. Add the chocolate and boil for 5 minutes: quickly at first, then more slowly. Remove from heat. Add orange extract and angelica. Stir until mixture thickens. Pour into prepared pan.

COCOA-CHOCOLATE FUDGE

Makes about 36 pieces

This recipe tastes like old-fashioned fudge that you'd buy in a candy store.

3 cups sugar
3 tbs. unsweetened cocoa powder, sifted
4 squares (1 oz. each) unsweetened chocolate

3 tbs. corn syrup
1 pinch salt
1 cup milk
3 tbs. butter, chopped
1 tsp. vanilla

Line an 8-inch square pan with foil. Melt sugar, cocoa, chocolate and corn syrup in a medium saucepan over medium heat; add salt and milk, stirring constantly. Brush sides of pan with pastry brush to prevent crystals from forming on sides of pan. Lower heat to medium-low and boil until mixture reaches 238° on a candy thermometer or until a small amount of syrup dropped into cold water can be formed into a soft ball. Pour into a bowl and beat with a mixer until fudge is a rich and smooth consistency. Pour into prepared pan. Refrigerate until firm.

SMOOTH CHOCOLATE FUDGE

Makes about 36 pieces

Sifting the dry ingredients helps to ensure a creamy consistency.

1 lb. confectioner's sugar
1/3 cup nonfat dry milk
4 tbs. (1/2 stick) butter
3 squares (1 oz. each) unsweetened chocolate

1/2 cup light or dark corn syrup
1 tbs. water
1 tsp. vanilla extract
1/2 cup chopped nuts

Line an 8-inch square pan with foil. Sift sugar and dry milk together; set aside. Melt butter and chocolate in top of a 2-quart double boiler or saucepan over boiling water. Stir corn syrup, water and vanilla into chocolate mixture over boiling water. Blend in dry ingredients, 1/2 at a time, stirring each time until mixture is blended and smooth. Remove from boiling water. Mix in nuts. Pour into prepared pan. Refrigerate until firm.

NOTE: if necessary, fudge may be prepared over low direct heat. Stir constantly while butter and chocolate are melting.

DOUBLE CHOCOLATE FUDGE

Makes about 80 pieces

For those of you who are super chocolate lovers, try this. It's so yummy!

1 pkg. (12 oz.) semisweet chocolate chips
1 can (14 oz.) sweetened condensed milk, divided
2 tsp. vanilla extract, divided
1 cup chopped walnuts, divided
1 pkg. (11½ oz.) milk chocolate chips

Line a 9-inch square pan with foil. In a heavy saucepan, melt semisweet chocolate chips with ½ cup plus 3 tbs. milk over low heat. Remove from heat; stir in 1 tsp. of the vanilla and ½ cup of the walnuts. Spread into prepared pan. In a separate saucepan, melt milk chocolate chips with remaining milk. Remove from the heat; stir in remaining vanilla and walnuts. Spread over first layer. Refrigerate until firm.

REAL CHOCOLATE FUDGE

Makes about 24 pieces

It takes some time to make, but I know you will love this one too!

2 cups sugar
$\frac{1}{8}$ tsp. salt
$\frac{3}{4}$ cup milk
2 squares (1 oz. each) unsweetened
   chocolate, chopped

4 tbs. ($\frac{1}{2}$ stick) butter
$\frac{1}{2}$ cup chopped nuts
2 tsp. vanilla extract

Line an 8 x 4-inch loaf pan with foil. In a large microwave-safe bowl stir sugar, salt and milk together. Add chocolate and butter. Microwave on high 6 minutes until hot and bubbly. Stir well. Microwave on medium-high 14 to 16 minutes, uncovered, stirring every 5 minutes, until mixture reaches 238° on a candy thermometer or until a small amount of syrup dropped into cold water can be formed into a soft ball. Remove from heat and cool to luke-warm. Quickly stir in nuts and pour into prepared pan. Refrigerate until firm.

CHOCOLATE CREAM FUDGE

Makes about 24 pieces

It's hard to believe this rich, creamy fudge contains no butter.

2 squares (1 oz. each) unsweetened chocolate
1 pkg. (3 oz.) cream cheese, softened
1 tsp. heavy cream
2 cups confectioner's sugar
1/2 tsp. vanilla
1 pinch salt
1 cup chopped nuts

Line an 8 x 4-inch loaf pan with foil. Melt chocolate in a double boiler or in the microwave; set aside. Beat cream cheese and cream in a medium bowl until smooth. Gradually beat in sugar. Add melted chocolate. Blend until smooth; add vanilla, salt and chopped nuts. Press into prepared pan. Refrigerate until firm.

CLASSIC FUDGE

Makes about 36 pieces

Here are a couple of ways to make classic fudge, both chocolate and old-fashioned vanilla, or "blonde" fudge.

2 oz. unsweetened chocolate	2 tbs. light or dark corn syrup
3 cups sugar	3 tbs. margarine
3/4 cup milk	1 tsp. vanilla extract

Line an 8-inch square pan with foil. In a heavy 3-quart saucepan combine chocolate, sugar, milk, and corn syrup. Bring to a boil over medium heat, stirring constantly. Reduce heat to medium-low and boil until mixture reaches 238° on a candy thermometer or until a small amount of syrup dropped into cold water can be formed into a soft ball. Remove from heat and add margarine and vanilla. DO NOT STIR. Cool to lukewarm. Beat until fudge begins to thicken and lose its gloss. Quickly pour into prepared pan. Refrigerate until firm. **For blonde fudge:** omit chocolate and increase corn syrup to 3 tbs. and vanilla to 2 tsp. Proceed as directed.

HONEY FUDGE

Makes about 36 pieces

My mom would love this, as it's not too sweet.

2 cups sugar
1 can (6 oz.) evaporated milk
1/4 cup honey
2 squares (1 oz. each) unsweetened
chocolate, grated

2 tbs. butter or margarine
1/8 tsp. salt
1 tsp. vanilla extract

Line an 8-inch square pan with foil. Cook sugar, milk and honey in a 2 1/2 quart saucepan over medium heat until sugar is dissolved. Stir in chocolate, butter and salt. Lower heat to medium-low. Boil until mixture reaches 238° on a candy thermometer or until a small amount of syrup dropped into cold water can be formed into a soft ball. Remove from heat and cool to lukewarm. Add vanilla and beat until mixture is thick and no longer glossy. Pour into prepared pan. Refrigerate until firm.

RICH COCOA FUDGE

Makes about 36 pieces

Using cocoa instead of chocolate chips will give this fudge a deeper rich chocolate taste. Note: for best results, do not double this recipe.

3 cups sugar
2/3 cup unsweetened cocoa powder
1/8 tsp. salt

1 1/2 cups milk
4 tbs. (1/2 stick) butter
1 tsp. vanilla extract

Line an 8-or 9-inch square pan with foil. In a heavy 4-quart saucepan, combine sugar, cocoa, and salt. Stir in milk. Cook over medium heat, stirring constantly until mixture comes to rolling boil. Lower heat to medium-low and boil until mixture reaches 238° on a candy thermometer or until a small amount of syrup dropped into cold water can be formed into a soft ball. Remove from heat and add butter and vanilla. DO NOT STIR. Cool to luke-warm. Beat with wooden spoon until fudge thickens and just begins to lose some of its gloss. Quickly spread into prepared pan. Refrigerate until firm.

NUTTY RICH COCOA FUDGE

Beat cooked fudge as directed. Immediately stir in 1 cup chopped almonds, pecans or walnuts and spread quickly into prepared pan.

MARSHMALLOW-NUT COCOA FUDGE

Increase cocoa to $3/4$ cup. Cook fudge as directed. Add 1 cup marshmallow crème with butter and vanilla. DO NOT STIR. Cool to 110°. Beat 8 minutes, stir in 1 cup chopped nuts. Pour into prepared pan. (Fudge does not set until poured into pan.)

DIVINITY FUDGE

Makes about 36 pieces

The first time I made this recipe, I couldn't believe how light the fudge turned out.

2 egg whites, at room temperature
$2^{1}/_{3}$ cups sugar
$^{2}/_{3}$ cup corn syrup
$^{1}/_{2}$ cup water
$^{1}/_{4}$ tsp. salt
$^{1}/_{2}$ tsp. vanilla extract

Line an 8-inch square pan with foil. In a large bowl, using a mixer, beat egg whites to stiff peaks; set aside. Mix sugar, corn syrup, water and salt into saucepan. Cook and stir over low heat until dissolved. Increase heat to medium-high. Cook, without stirring, to 265° on a candy thermometer, or until a small amount dropped into cold water forms a hard ball.

As syrup cooks, wipe the crystals from sides of pan with a wet pastry brush. Gradually pour hot syrup over egg whites in a thin stream, beating constantly at high speed until stiff peaks form when beater is raised. Stir in vanilla. Pour into prepared pan. While still warm, cut into squares.

ORANGE DIVINITY
Substitute 3 tbs. grated orange zest for the vanilla.

ALMOND DIVINITY
Substitute almond extract for the vanilla. Add $1/3$ cup blanched, chopped almonds.

PENUCHE

Makes about 64 pieces

I never knew what penuche was until I made this recipe. The brown sugar gives it a unique nutty flavor.

$1/2$ cup light corn syrup
$1\,1/2$ tsp. butter
2 cups brown sugar, packed
$1/2$ cup milk
$1/4$ tsp. salt
$1/3$ tsp. vanilla extract

Line an 8-inch square pan with foil. Combine corn syrup, butter, sugar, milk and salt in a medium saucepan. Bring to a boil over medium-low heat, stirring constantly. Boil until mixture reaches 238° on a candy thermometer or until a small amount of syrup dropped into cold water can be formed into a soft ball. Remove from heat and cool to lukewarm. Add vanilla. Mix well. Refrigerate until firm. Store in refrigerator.

WONDER FUDGE

Makes about 36 pieces

The Rice Krispies in this recipe make the fudge taste like a Nestlé Crunch Bar.

4 tbs. (¹/₂ stick) margarine or butter
1 pkg. (6 oz.) semisweet chocolate chips
¹/₄ cup corn syrup
1 tsp. vanilla extract
1¹/₂ cups sifted confectioner's sugar
2 cups Rice Krispies cereal

Line an 8-inch square pan with foil. Combine margarine, chocolate, corn syrup and vanilla in a large saucepan. Cook over very low heat, stirring constantly, until smooth. Remove from heat and stir in sugar. Add Rice Krispies. and stir until evenly coated. Press mixture in prepared pan. Refrigerate until firm.

GOLDEN FUDGE

Makes about 36 pieces

A little bit of gold always comes in handy.

3 cups sugar
1/4 cup light corn syrup
3 tbs. butter or margarine
1/2 tsp. salt

1 cup evaporated milk
1/2 cup water
2 tsp. vanilla extract
slivered candied cherries for garnish

Line an 8-inch square pan with foil. Combine sugar, corn syrup, butter, salt, evaporated milk and water in a heavy saucepan over medium heat. Bring to a rolling boil, stirring constantly. Reduce heat to medium-low and boil until mixture reaches 238° on a candy thermometer or until a small amount of syrup dropped into cold water can be formed into a soft ball. Remove from heat and add vanilla. DO NOT STIR. Cool to lukewarm. Beat for 2 to 3 minutes, or until it starts to thicken and is no longer glossy. Spread in prepared pan, let stand for 2 to 3 minutes, or just until set. Cut into squares. Decorate each piece with a cherry sliver. Let stand until firm.

CREAM CHEESE FUDGE

Makes about 24 pieces

The cream cheese makes this fudge so creamy, you might want to put it on a bagel instead.

1 pkg. (3 oz.) cream cheese, cut in pieces
1/2 cup butterscotch chips
1 tsp. milk

2 cups sifted confectioner's sugar
1/4 tsp vanilla
1 pinch salt
1 cup miniature marshmallows

Line an 8 x 4-inch loaf pan with foil. In a 1-quart microwave-safe bowl, place cream cheese, butterscotch chips and milk. Cover and cook on high for 1 minute, or until melted. Stir once. Stir in sugar, vanilla and salt. Fold in marshmallows. Immediately pour into prepared pan. Refrigerate until firm.

GRAHAM CRACKER FUDGE

Makes about 72 pieces

When I first read the ingredients to this fudge, I couldn't wait to make it!

2 cups sugar
2 oz. unsweetened chocolate
1 cup cream
1 lb. miniature marshmallows

2 cups crushed graham crackers
1 cup chopped nuts
2 tbs. butter
1 tsp. vanilla

Line two 8-inch square pans with foil. Combine sugar, chocolate and cream in a large saucepan. Cook over medium heat, stirring constantly, until mixture begins to boil. Cook without stirring, keeping heat just high enough to prevent mixture from boiling over. Wash down sides of saucepan occasionally with a damp pastry brush to prevent crystals from forming. Boil until mixture reaches 238° on a candy thermometer or until a small amount of syrup dropped into cold water can be formed into a soft ball. Remove from heat. Add marshmallows, graham crackers, nuts, butter and vanilla. Mix well. Pour at once into pans. Refrigerate until firm.

ROCKY ROAD FUDGE

Makes about 90 pieces

This recipe has been around at least since the beginning of time. Rocky road candy bars are my Mom's favorite, so this one is for her. Here's to you, Mom!

1 pkg. (16 oz.) chocolate chips
2 tbs. butter
1 can (14 oz.) sweetened
  condensed milk

1 cup lightly salted peanuts
1 cup miniature marshmallows
1 jar (6 oz.) maraschino cherries,
  halved

Line a 9 x 13-inch pan with foil. Melt chocolate in a medium saucepan over low heat, stirring often. Remove from heat. Stir in butter until melted, then milk until blended. Stir in peanuts, marshmallows and cherries. Spread in prepared pan. Refrigerate until firm.

MARBLE FUDGE

Makes about 36 pieces

This fudge looks like a marble cake, and it's quick and easy to make. Remember to sift the sugar.

1 cup confectioner's sugar	1/4 cup corn syrup
3/4 cup peanut butter, divided	1/2 tsp. vanilla extract
4 tbs. (1/2 stick) butter, softened	1/4 cup chocolate chips, melted

Line an 8-inch square pan with foil. Sift confectioner's sugar into a small bowl; set aside. In a separate bowl, beat together 1/2 cup of the peanut butter, butter, corn syrup and vanilla. Stir in confectioner's sugar until well blended. Pour into prepared pan; set aside. Melt chocolate in a glass cup in the microwave. Swirl chocolate into remaining peanut butter for a marbled effect. Pour into prepared pan and refrigerate until firm.

FRUIT FUDGE

Makes about 36 pieces

You can also add chopped dates with the figs and raisins, like my grand-mother's favorite version of this chewy, sweet fudge.

1/2 cup milk	1/4 cup chopped nuts
2 cups sugar	1/4 cup chopped dried figs
2 tbs. butter	1/4 cup chopped raisins
1 tsp. lemon or orange extract	

Line an 8-inch square pan with foil. Combine milk and sugar in a saucepan over medium heat. Bring to a boil. Boil until mixture reaches 238° on a candy thermometer or until a small amount of syrup dropped into cold water can be formed into a soft ball. Add butter and extract. Remove from heat. Beat until creamy. Quickly add nuts and fruit. Pour into prepared pan. Refrigerate until firm.

CHOCO-CHERRY COCONUT FUDGE

Makes about 36 pieces

This double-decker fudge is packed with cherries and coconut.

$2/3$ cup vanilla chips
$1/2$ cup dried tart cherries, chopped
$1\,1/4$ cups sweetened condensed milk

2 tbs. butter
2 cups chocolate chips
$1/2$ cup coconut, divided

Line an 8-inch square pan with foil. Place vanilla chips and cherries in a bowl; set aside. In a saucepan over low heat, heat milk and butter until butter is melted. Measure out $2/3$ cup and mix with vanilla chips in bowl until chips are melted. Add chocolate chips to remaining mixture in saucepan and stir until melted.

Drop half the vanilla-cherry mixture by spoonfuls into prepared pan, leaving spaces between. Sprinkle with half the coconut. Spread chocolate mixture evenly on top, and then spoon on remaining vanilla mixture. Sprinkle with remaining coconut. Refrigerate until firm.

STRAWBERRY FUDGE

Makes about 36 pieces

My grandchildren always beg me for this one. I stir in a few chopped fresh strawberries with the marshmallows on the top of the fudge while it's still hot.

2³/₄ cups sugar
2 tbs. margarine
1 can (6 oz.) evaporated milk
2 cups miniature marshmallows
1 cup finely chopped pecans
2 tbs. strawberry flavored gelatin powder

Line an 8-inch square pan with foil. Mix sugar, margarine and milk in a saucepan over medium heat. Bring to a rolling boil, stirring constantly. Boil for 5 minutes, stirring constantly. Remove from heat and stir in marshmallows. When melted, stir in nuts and gelatin. Pour into prepared dish. Refrigerate until firm.

LUSCIOUS FIG FUDGE

Makes about 36 pieces

I love the taste of the the figs in this one, and I think you will, too.

3 cups sugar
1 cup milk
3 tbs. light corn syrup
3 tbs. butter

1 tsp. vanilla extract
1/2 cup chopped dried figs
1/2 cup chopped pecans

Line an 8-inch square pan with foil. In medium saucepan heat sugar, milk and corn syrup to boiling, stirring frequently until sugar is dissolved. Boil until mixture reaches 238° on a candy thermometer or until a small amount of syrup dropped into cold water can be formed into a soft ball. Remove from heat and add butter and vanilla. DO NOT STIR. Cool mixture to lukewarm. With a wooden spoon beat until fudge is thick and no longer glossy. Quickly, stir in figs and pecans. Pour fudge into pan. Refrigerate until firm.

CHERRY CREAM FUDGE

Makes about 36 pieces

Make sure to use candied cherries to experience the terrific taste.

4 cups sugar	2 tsp. white vinegar
1 cup half-and-half	2 tsp. vanilla extract
1/2 cup light corn syrup	1/2 cup marshmallow crème
1/2 tsp. salt	1 cup pecans
1 cup (2 sticks) butter or margarine	1 cup candied cherries

Line an 8-inch square pan with foil. In a heavy 4-quart saucepan over medium heat, combine sugar, half-and-half, corn syrup, salt, butter and vinegar. Bring to a boil, stirring constantly until sugar is dissolved. Reduce heat to low. Boil until mixture reaches 238° on a candy thermometer or until a small amount of syrup dropped into cold water can be formed into a soft ball. Remove from heat. Add vanilla and marshmallow crème. Mix well. Add pecans and cherries. Spread in prepared pan. Refrigerate until firm.

CHERRY DIVINITY FUDGE

Makes about 12 pieces

Remember when you thought divinity was only a candy? Now you can make it into a fudge that's perfect to serve during the holidays.

3 egg whites, at room temperature
$1/4$ tsp. salt
3 cups sugar
$2/3$ cup light corn syrup
$3/4$ cup water
1 tsp. vanilla extract
2 cups coarsely chopped pecans or walnuts
6 candied cherries, quartered
6 candied cherries, halved, for garnish
12 pecans, for garnish

Line an 11 x 7-inch pan with foil. Place egg whites into large bowl of electric mixer. Add salt and beat egg whites until stiff peaks form; set aside.

In a heavy 3-quart saucepan, combine sugar, corn syrup and water. Cook, stirring, over low heat to dissolve sugar. Cover; cook 1 minute longer to dissolve sugar crystals on sides of pan.

Uncover; raise heat to medium and boil without stirring to 260° on a candy thermometer, or until a small amount placed in cold water forms a firm ball. Set aside to cool slightly.

When thermometer goes down to 250°, gradually pour hot syrup over egg whites in a thin stream, beating constantly at high speed until stiff peaks form when beater is raised, about 5 minutes. Using a wooden spoon, beat in vanilla, chopped nuts and quartered cherries. Continue beating until mixture is stiff enough to hold its shape and looks dull. Turn into prepared pan. Refrigerate until firm. Top each piece with a cherry half or nut.

CRANBERRY OPERA FUDGE

Makes about 30 pieces

I love tangy cranberries, and the contrast with the sweet fudge is a special treat.

2 cups sugar
$^1/_2$ cup milk
$^1/_2$ cup light cream
1 tbs. light corn syrup

$^1/_2$ tsp. salt
1 tbs. butter or margarine
1 tsp. vanilla extract
$^1/_2$ cup fresh cranberries, chopped

Line a 9 x 5-inch loaf pan with foil. Butter sides of a heavy 2-quart saucepan. In it combine sugar, milk, cream, corn syrup and salt. Boil until mixture reaches 238° on a candy thermometer or until a small amount of syrup dropped into cold water can be formed into a soft ball. Remove from heat and add butter and vanilla. DO NOT STIR. Cool to lukewarm. Beat vigorously until mixture becomes very thick and starts to lose its gloss. Quickly stir in cranberries and spread in prepared pan. Refrigerate until firm.

FRUITED FUDGES

FUDGEMALLOW RAISIN CANDY

Makes about 36 pieces

Now we can have the chunky candy we used to get when we were kids!

1 pkg. (12 oz.) semisweet chocolate chips
1 cup chunky style peanut butter
3 cups miniature marshmallows
3/4 cup raisins

Line an 8-inch square pan with foil. Melt chocolate chips with peanut butter in a saucepan over low heat, stirring until smooth. Fold in marshmallows and raisins. Pour into prepared pan. Refrigerate until firm.

CRANBERRY WALNUT WHITE FUDGE

Makes about 36 pieces

You'll love the combination of white chocolate and cranberries.

2 cups sugar
3/4 cup sour cream
1/2 cup (1 stick) butter (no substitutes)
10–12 oz. vanilla or white chocolate chips

1 jar (7 oz.) marshmallow crème
1 tsp. vanilla extract
3 cups walnuts, coarsely chopped
1 cup dried cranberries, coarsely chopped

Line an 8-inch square pan with foil. In a heavy saucepan, bring sugar, sour cream and butter to a boil over medium heat. Boil until mixture reaches 238° on a candy thermometer or until a small amount of syrup dropped into cold water can be formed into a soft ball. Remove from heat. Stir in chips, marshmallow crème and vanilla until smooth. Fold in walnuts and cranberries. Pour into prepared pan. Refrigerate until firm.

WHITE CHRISTMAS FUDGE

Makes about 36 pieces

Bing Crosby would have loved this! Sour cream gives it a creamy texture.

2½ cups sugar
½ cup sour cream
¼ cup milk
2 tbs. butter
1 tbs. light corn syrup

¼ tsp. salt
1 tsp. vanilla extract
1 cup walnuts, coarsely chopped
⅓ cup quartered candied cherries

Line an 8-inch square pan with foil. Combine sugar, sour cream, milk, butter, corn syrup and salt in a heavy 2-quart saucepan. Stir over medium heat until sugar is dissolved and mixture reaches a boil. Boil until mixture reaches 238° on a candy thermometer or until a small amount of syrup dropped into cold water can be formed into a soft ball. Remove from heat and cool to lukewarm. Add vanilla and beat well until mixture just begins to lose its gloss and thicken. Quickly stir in walnuts and cherries and pour into prepared pan. Refrigerate until firm.

HOLIDAY HARLEQUIN FUDGE

Makes about 36 pieces

With candied cherries and nuts, this recipe is perfect for Christmas—like fruitcake, but so much tastier!

1 pkg. (6 oz.) semisweet chocolate chips
1/2 cup chopped walnuts
3/4 cup chopped white chocolate
1/4 cup chopped red candied cherries
1 1/3 cups sugar
1/3 cup brandy or pineapple juice
1/2 cup sour cream
2 tbs. butter
16 large marshmallows, quartered
1/4 tsp. salt

Line a 9 x 5-inch loaf pan with foil. Place semisweet chocolate and walnuts in a bowl; set aside. Place white chocolate and cherries in a separate bowl; set aside. Combine sugar, brandy, sour cream, butter, marshmallows and salt in a heavy saucepan. Cook, stirring, over medium heat until sugar is dissolved. Lower heat to medium-low and boil until mixture reaches 238° on a candy thermometer or until a small amount of syrup dropped into cold water can be formed into a soft ball. Remove from heat. Working quickly, pour about ³/₄ cup of the hot mixture into chocolate-walnut mixture and stir until chocolate is melted. Pour into prepared pan. Pour remaining hot syrup into white chocolate-cherry mixture and stir until chocolate is melted. Pour into pan over chocolate-walnut mixture and quickly spread level. Refrigerate until firm.

FANTASY FUDGE

Makes about 90 pieces

Making this fudge during the holidays has been a tradition for my mom and me since I was a little girl.

3 cups sugar
³/₄ cup margarine
1 can (6 oz.) evaporated milk
1 pkg. (12 oz.) chocolate chips

1 jar (7 oz.) marshmallow crème
1 cup chopped nuts
1 tsp. vanilla extract

Line a 9 x 13-inch pan with foil. Combine sugar, margarine and milk in heavy 3-quart saucepan. Bring to a rolling boil over medium heat, stirring constantly. Boil 5 minutes, stirring constantly. Remove from heat. Stir in chocolate until melted. Add marshmallow crème, nuts and vanilla extract. Beat until well blended. Pour into prepared pan. Refrigerate until firm.

EGGNOG FUDGE

Makes about 24 pieces

Save a little eggnog for sipping while making your fudge.

2 cups sugar
1 cup eggnog
1 tbs. light corn syrup
2 tbs. butter plus 1 tsp.

1 tsp. vanilla extract
1/2 cup chopped walnuts
2 tbs. semisweet chocolate chips

Line an 8 x 4-inch pan with foil. Butter sides of a heavy saucepan and add sugar, eggnog, and corn syrup. Cook over medium heat, stirring constantly, until sugar dissolves and mixture comes to a boil. Lower heat to medium-low and boil until mixture reaches 238° on a candy thermometer. Remove from heat and cool to lukewarm. Add 2 tbs. of the butter and vanilla. Beat vigorously until fudge becomes very thick and loses its gloss. Quickly stir in nuts. Spread in prepared pan. In a glass measuring cup, combine chocolate and remaining 1 tsp. butter. Microwave on high 30 seconds or just until melted. Drizzle over top of fudge. Refrigerate until firm.

CHOCOLATE SNOW FUDGE

Makes about 36 pieces

Even the title makes your mouth water. I prefer to use heavy Hershey's syrup in this recipe.

1 lb. confectioner's sugar
$1/2$ cup nonfat dry milk
1 cup chocolate flavored syrup
$1/4$ cup margarine
1 tsp. vanilla extract
$1/2$ cup coarsely chopped nuts

Line an 8-inch square pan with foil. Sift confectioner's sugar and non-fat dry milk together. In a small saucepan, bring chocolate syrup to a boil. Remove from heat. Stir in margarine. Stir in sugar mixture about $1/3$ at a time. Continue stirring until fudge is thick and smooth. Stir in vanilla and nuts. Pour into prepared pan. Refrigerate until firm. Sprinkle with extra confectioners' sugar, for the "snow."

CHRISTMAS LIGHT FUDGE

Makes about 64 pieces

The gum drops in this one give it that extra holiday look that will be sure to light up your table.

1/3 cup butter or margarine
3 squares (1 oz. each) unsweetened chocolate
1/2 cup milk
1/2 cup creamy peanut butter

2 tsp. vanilla extract
1/8 tsp. salt
1 pound confectioner's sugar, sifted
64 gum drops

Line an 8-inch square pan with foil. Heat butter, chocolate and milk in a medium saucepan over low heat until melted, stirring constantly. Remove from heat. Add peanut butter, vanilla, salt, and about 1/2 of the sugar; stir until smooth. Beat in remaining sugar. Spread mixture in prepared pan. Refrigerate until firm. Press a gum drop on top of each piece.

PEPPERMINT CHOCOLATE FUDGE

Makes about 36 pieces

Peppermint lovers are going to love this recipe!

1 pkg. (12 oz.) milk chocolate chips
1 pkg. (6 oz.) semisweet chocolate chips
1 can (14 oz.) sweetened condensed milk
1 pinch salt
$1/2$ tsp. peppermint extract
1 cup crushed hard peppermint candy

Line an 8-inch square pan with foil. In saucepan, over low heat, melt both chocolates, sweetened condensed milk and salt. Remove from heat and stir in peppermint extract. Spread evenly into prepared pan. Sprinkle with peppermint candy and press into fudge. Refrigerate until firm.

HOLIDAY FUDGE

Makes about 60 pieces

The red and green in the white fudge will make any table the talk of the town!

3 cups sugar
1 cup corn syrup
1 1/2 cups light cream
1 1/2 tsp. vanilla extract

3/4 cup chopped walnuts
3/4 cup pecan halves
1 cup candied cherries, diced
1 cup candied pineapple, diced

Line an 8-inch square pan with foil. Lightly oil a large, heavy-bottomed saucepan and add sugar, corn syrup and cream. Cook over low heat, stirring until the sugar is dissolved. Increase the heat to medium and bring to a boil, stirring occasionally. Boil until mixture reaches 238° on a candy thermometer or until a small amount of syrup dropped into cold water can be formed into a soft ball. Remove from heat. Beat immediately until it begins to lose its gloss and starts to thicken. Add vanilla. Slowly stir in nuts and fruit. Refrigerate until firm.

PUMPKIN NUT FUDGE

Makes about 36 pieces

This fudge will make you think you were eating a homemade pumpkin pie without the crust.

4 cups sugar
1/2 cup light corn syrup
1 pinch salt
1 1/3 cups milk
4 tbs. (1/2 stick) butter, chopped

2 tbs. pumpkin puree
1/4 tsp. pumpkin spice
1/4–1/2 cup chopped walnuts or
      pecans, optional

Line an 8-inch square pan with foil. In a saucepan over medium heat, combine sugar, syrup, salt and milk. Stir until sugar is dissolved, then boil without stirring until mixture reaches 238° on a candy thermometer. Fudge should be a caramel color. Remove from heat and add butter, pumpkin and pumpkin spice. DO NOT STIR. Cool to lukewarm. Beat vigorously until mixture is smooth and glossy. Fold in nuts, if using, and sprinkle a few on top. Refrigerate until firm.

NO-COOK PEANUT BUTTER FUDGE

Makes about 60 pieces

Fast and easy, this fudge doesn't require a candy thermometer, or even a saucepan.

$1/2$ cup honey or light corn syrup
$1/2$ cup (1 stick) butter or margarine, softened
$3/4$ cup crunchy peanut butter
$1/2$ cup dry skim milk powder
$1/2$ tsp. salt
1 tsp. vanilla extract
1 pound confectioner's sugar, sifted

Line an 8-inch square pan with foil. Combine honey, butter, peanut butter, powdered milk, salt, vanilla and confectioner's sugar in a large bowl. Knead with your hands until well blended. Press evenly in prepared pan. Refrigerate until firm.

FOOLPROOF CHOCOLATE FUDGE

Makes about 60 pieces

Fudge can't get any easier than making it in the microwave.

3 pkg. (6 oz. each) semisweet
   chocolate chips
1 can (14 oz.) sweetened
   condensed milk

1 pinch salt
3/4 cup chopped nuts

Line an 8-inch square pan with foil. In a glass bowl or 1-quart measuring cup, combine chocolate with sweetened condensed milk. Microwave on high for 3 minutes, stopping halfway to stir, until chocolate melts and mixture is smooth. Stir in salt and nuts. Spread evenly in prepared pan. Refrigerate until firm.

FOOLPROOF CREAMY DARK FUDGE

Add 2 cups miniature marshmallows with chips and milk. Proceed as above.

FOOLPROOF MILK CHOCOLATE FUDGE

Substitute 1 cup milk chocolate chips for one 6-oz. package semisweet chips. Proceed as above

FOOLPROOF CREAMY MILK CHOCOLATE FUDGE

Substitute 1 cup milk chocolate chips and 2 cups miniature marshmallows for the semisweet chips. Proceed as above.

FOOLPROOF MEXICAN FUDGE

Reduce vanilla to 1 tsp. Add 1 tbs. instant coffee powder and 1 tsp. cinnamon to condensed milk. Proceed as above.

FOOLPROOF BUTTERSCOTCH FUDGE

Substitute one 12-oz. package butterscotch chips for the semisweet chocolate. Omit vanilla and stir in 2 tbs. white vinegar, 1 tsp. maple extract and 1 cup chopped nuts to melted chips-milk mixture. Proceed as above.

SPEEDY PEANUT BUTTER CUP FUDGE

Makes about 60 pieces

Your kids will love the peanut butter-chocolate combo. The cream really makes for a smooth texture.

3/4 cup smooth or crunchy peanut butter
1 pkg. (6 oz.) semisweet chocolate chips
2 cups miniature marshmallows
1/4 cup heavy cream or milk
1 tsp. vanilla extract

Line an 8-inch square pan with foil. In a 2-quart glass bowl, combine peanut butter, chocolate chips, marshmallows, cream and vanilla. Microwave on high 1 1/2 to 2 minutes, or until chocolate and marshmallows are melted and mixture is smooth when stirred. Pour into prepared pan. Cool 1/2 hour, then refrigerate until firm.

MILK CHOCOLATE FUDGE

Makes about 36 pieces

Have a nice big glass of milk on hand when having this one.

1 pkg. (12 oz.) milk chocolate chips
1 cup sweetened condensed milk
3 tbs. butter

2 tsp. vanilla extract
$^3/_4$ cup walnuts, chopped

Line an 8-inch square pan with foil. Place chocolate in a microwave-safe dish or measuring cup. Microwave, uncovered, on medium-high 1$^1/_2$ minutes. Stir and continue microwaving, checking every 30 seconds, until chocolate is just melted. Stir in condensed milk, butter and vanilla. Blend until butter is melted and mixture is smooth. Stir in nuts. Spread into prepared pan. Cool at room temperature.

NOTE: Chocolate can be melted in top of a double boiler over very low heat. Stir until melted.

QUICK DARK CHOCOLATE FUDGE

Makes about 60 pieces

This fudge is quick and easy for working moms who don't have much time. Try using milk chocolate instead of semisweet, if desired.

3 pkg. (6 oz. each) semisweet
   chocolate chips
1 can (14 oz.) sweetened
   condensed milk

1 pinch salt
1/2–1 cup chopped nuts
1 1/2 tsp. vanilla extract

Line an 8-inch square pan with foil. In a heavy saucepan over low heat, melt chocolate with condensed milk and salt. Remove from heat; stir in nuts and vanilla. Spread evenly into prepared pan. Refrigerate until firm.

MICROWAVE INSTRUCTIONS

In 1-quart glass measure, combine chocolate with condensed milk and salt. Cook on high for 3 minutes or until chocolate is melted, stirring after 1 1/2 minutes. Add remaining ingredients. Proceed as above.

MICROWAVE CHOCOLATE FUDGE

Makes about 90 pieces

This fudge is to die for!

3/4 cup butter or margarine
3 cups sugar
1 can (6 oz.) evaporated milk
3 squares (1 oz. each) unsweetened
    chocolate, finely chopped

2 cups semisweet chocolate chips
1 jar (7 oz.) marshmallow crème
1 cup walnuts, coarsely chopped
2 tsp. vanilla extract

Line a 9 x 13-inch baking dish with foil. In a large microwave-safe bowl, microwave butter on high 30 seconds, or until melted. Stir in sugar and milk. Microwave uncovered on high for 10 to 12 minutes, stirring and scraping down sides every 3 minutes. When mixture boils rapidly, remove from microwave and immediately stir in both chocolates until melted. Stir in marshmallow crème, nuts and vanilla. Spread in prepared dish. Refrigerate until firm.

COFFEE-WALNUT FUDGE

Makes about 36 pieces

Pour yourself a cup of java and have a piece of this fabulous fudge!

3 cups sugar
1 cup half-and-half
3 tbs. light corn syrup
1/4 tsp. salt
1 tbs. instant coffee powder
2 tsp. hot water
4 tbs. (1/2 stick) butter or margarine
1/4 tsp. vanilla extract
1 cup chopped walnuts

Line an 8-inch square pan with foil. In a 5-quart microwave-safe bowl, combine sugar, half-and-half, corn syrup and salt. Microwave on high 5 to 7 minutes, until mixture comes to full boil, stirring occasionally.

NUT FUDGES

Continue to microwave on high until mixture reaches 238° on a candy thermometer or until a small amount of syrup dropped into cold water can be formed into a soft ball. Do not leave thermometer in microwave. Dissolve coffee in hot water. Add coffee, butter, and vanilla to hot mixture. do not stir. Cool to lukewarm. When mixture is cool, beat with wooden spoon until fudge becomes thick and is no longer glossy. Stir in nuts. Pour fudge into prepared pan. Refrigerate until firm.

PISTACHIO LEMON FUDGE

Makes about 50 pieces

The cream and the white chocolate make this the most heavenly fudge. Try adding a bit of grated lemon zest for a more lemony flavor.

1 lb. white chocolate, chopped	1 cup chopped unsalted pistachios
1 cup sifted confectioner's sugar	1 tbs. heavy cream
1 cup corn syrup	1 tbs. fresh lemon juice
1/4 cup (1/2 stick) butter or margarine	1 tsp. vanilla extract

Line a 9 x 13-inch pan with foil. Combine chocolate, confectioner's sugar, corn syrup and butter in a 2-quart microwave-safe bowl. Do not stir. Microwave on high for 3 minutes, stirring after 1 1/2 minutes. Beat until chocolate melts and mixture is smooth. Add pistachios, cream, lemon juice and vanilla, stirring until smooth. Pour mixture into prepared pan, spreading with a spatula to form an even layer. Refrigerate until firm.

NUT FUDGES

BRAZIL NUT FUDGE

Makes about 60 pieces

Made with brown sugar and cream, this one just can't get any better!

3 cups sugar
2 cups brown sugar, packed
2 cups heavy cream
4 squares unsweetened chocolate,
    coarsely chopped

1/4 cup dark corn syrup
4 tbs. butter or margarine
2 tsp. vanilla
1 1/2 cups brazil nuts, coarsely
    chopped

Line an 8-inch square pan with foil. In a heavy 4-quart saucepan, over medium heat, bring sugar, brown sugar, cream, chocolate and corn syrup to a boil, stirring constantly. Boil until mixture reaches 238° on a candy thermometer. Remove saucepan from heat and immediately pour mixture in a large bowl. Don't scrape saucepan: mixture on sides may be grainy. Add butter and vanilla. DO NOT STIR. Cool to lukewarm. With spoon, beat mixture until it becomes thick and is no longer glossy. Quickly stir in nuts; pour into pan. Refrigerate until firm.

MACADAMIA NUT FUDGE

Makes about 36 pieces

I buy macadamia nuts in bulk because they are expensive. That way I can make double batches of this fudge, one for home and one for work.

1/2 cup (1 stick) unsalted butter, cut into pieces
1 pkg. (6 oz.) semisweet chocolate chips
1 cup coarsely chopped macadamia nuts
1 square (1 oz.) unsweetened chocolate, finely chopped
1 tsp. vanilla
2 1/4 cups sugar
1 can (6 oz.) evaporated milk
12 large marshmallows

Line an 8-inch square pan with foil. In a large bowl combine butter, chocolate chips, nuts, unsweetened chocolate and vanilla; set aside. In a saucepan place sugar, milk and marshmallows. Bring to a boil over medium heat, stirring constantly to prevent burning. Boil until mixture reaches 238° on a candy thermometer or until a small amount of syrup dropped into cold water can be formed into a soft ball. Pour the hot mixture over the chocolate mixture in the bowl and let stand for 30 minutes. Stir until the mixture thickens. Spread in prepared pan. Refrigerate until firm.

BRAZIL NUT FUDGE SLICES

Makes about 32 pieces

The old-fashioned method of rolling out fudge in a log looks very impressive, but is really very easy to do.

2 cups sugar
1 cup maple syrup
1 cup milk
2 oz. unsweetened chocolate

1 pinch salt
2 tbs. butter or margarine
1 tsp. vanilla
1 cup coarsely chopped brazil nuts

Butter sides of a heavy 3-quart saucepan and add sugar, syrup, milk, chocolate and salt. Cook, stirring, over medium heat until sugar dissolves and mixture comes to a boil. Boil until mixture reaches 238° on a candy thermometer. Remove from heat, add butter and cool to lukewarm. DO NOT STIR. Add vanilla. Beat until mixture begins to lose its gloss. Stir in nuts. Spoon onto buttered baking sheet. Shape with buttered hands into two 8-inch-long logs. Refrigerate until firm. Slice when firm, or wrap unsliced logs in waxed paper and store at room temperature.

MACADAMIA ORANGE FUDGE

Makes about 90 pieces

This recipe is great for summer barbecues or luaus.

3 cups sugar
³/₄ cup (1¹/₂ sticks) butter
1 can (6 oz.) evaporated milk
1 pkg. (l2 oz.) semisweet chocolate chips
1 jar (7 oz.) marshmallow crème
1 cup macadamia nuts
2 tbs. orange flavored liqueur

Line a 9 x 13-inch pan with foil. In heavy saucepan combine sugar, butter and milk. Bring to a rolling boil over medium heat, stirring constantly. Boil 5 minutes, stirring constantly. Remove from heat. Add chocolate chips; stir until smooth. Add marshmallow crème, nuts and orange liqueur; beat until well blended. Pour into prepared pan. Refrigerate until firm.

DOUBLE-DECKER FUDGE

Makes about 64 pieces

The sour cream makes this fudge light and airy with a creamy texture.

2 cups sugar
1 cup sour cream
2 tbs. butter or margarine
1 pinch salt
3 tbs. unsweetened cocoa powder

$^{1}/_{2}$ cup water
1 cup chopped nuts
1 can sweetened condensed milk
1 pkg. (12 oz.) peanut butter chips
1 tsp. vanilla extract

Line an 8-inch square pan with foil. In a saucepan, combine sugar, sour cream, butter and salt. Butter sides of pan. Mix cocoa and water and stir into saucepan. Bring to a boil. Boil until mixture reaches 238° on a candy thermometer or until a small amount of syrup dropped into cold water can be formed into a soft ball. Remove from heat and cool to lukewarm. Stir in nuts and beat until mixture just starts to thicken. Spread into prepared pan. In a separate saucepan over medium heat, combine condensed milk and chips. Stir until smooth and melted. Stir in vanilla and spread mixture evenly over cocoa fudge. Refrigerate until firm.

PEANUT BUTTER FUDGE

Makes about 90 pieces

A favorite of kids big and small. Try melting about 1/2 cup chocolate chips and spreading the melted chocolate on top.

3 cups sugar
3/4 cup (1 1/2 sticks) butter
1 can (6 oz.) evaporated milk
1 pkg. (12 oz.) peanut butter chips

1 jar (7 oz.) marshmallow crème
1 tsp. vanilla extract
1/2 cup chopped peanuts

Line an 9 x 13-inch pan with foil. In a heavy saucepan, combine sugar, butter and milk. Bring to a rolling boil over medium heat, stirring constantly. Boil 5 minutes, stirring constantly. Remove from heat. Add peanut butter chips and stir until chips are melted and mixture is smooth. Add marshmallow crème and vanilla and beat until smooth. Pour into prepared pan. Sprinkle with nuts and press into fudge. Refrigerate until firm.

CHOCOLATE PECAN FUDGE

Makes about 16 pieces

Loaded with pecans, this fudge is a nut lover's dream.

2¹/₂ cups sugar
1 jar (7 oz.) marshmallow crème
³/₄ cup evaporated milk
¹/₂ cup (1 stick) butter (no
  substitutes) butter or margarine

1 pkg. (12 oz.) semisweet chocolate
  chips
¹/₂ cup chopped pecans
1 tsp. vanilla
16 pecan halves

Line an 8-inch square pan with foil. In a saucepan over medium heat combine sugar, marshmallow crème, milk and butter. Bring to a boil, stirring constantly. Reduce the heat to medium-low and boil gently for 7 minutes. Remove from heat. With a wooden spoon, beat in chocolate, chopped pecans and vanilla until well blended. Pour into prepared pan. With tip of sharp knife, mark off 2-inch squares and press a pecan half in center of each. Refrigerate until firm.

CREAMY CHOCOLATE-PECAN FUDGE   Makes about 100 pieces

This fudge hardens quickly, so don't dilly-dally when you put it in the pan.

8 squares (1 oz. each) semisweet
    chocolate, coarsely chopped
8 squares (1 oz. each) unsweetened
    chocolate, coarsely chopped
7 1/2 oz. jar marshmallow crème
2 cups pecans, coarsely chopped

1 can (13 oz.) evaporated milk
4 cups sugar
2 tbs. butter or margarine
1/4 tsp. salt
1 tbs. vanilla
pecan halves, for garnish

Line a 15 x 10 x 1-inch pan with foil. Place both chocolates, marshmallow crème and pecans in a large bowl; set aside. In a large heavy saucepan over medium-low heat combine milk, sugar, butter and salt. Bring to boil and boil slowly for 9 minutes, stirring constantly. Pour at once over chocolate mixture; add vanilla. With a wooden spoon, stir vigorously until chocolate is melted and mixture is creamy. Pour into prepared pan. Garnish with pecan halves. Refrigerate until firm.

FUDGE A LA LOUISE

Makes about 90 pieces

There is a lot of work to this fudge but let me tell you it is well worth the work and the wait.

4 cups sugar
3 squares (1 oz. each) unsweetened chocolate, chopped
1$\frac{1}{3}$ cups milk
2 tbs. butter
1$\frac{1}{3}$ tsp. vanilla extract
1 cup chopped nuts

Butter a large platter (turkey size) and a flat pan about 11 x 13 inches. In a heavy saucepan mix together the sugar, chocolate and milk. Place the pan over high heat and cook, stirring constantly, until the chocolate is melted and the sugar is dissolved. Bring to a rolling boil and lower the heat so the candy continues to boil gently, not vigorously. Do not stir. Cook until the temperature on a candy thermometer reaches exactly 232°.

Immediately pour mixture onto the prepared platter—do not scrape the pan. Dot with butter and set platter aside cool until the platter feels cool underneath. Add vanilla. Using a large slotted spoon, stir the mixture for about 15 to 20 minutes until the fudge thickens and turns from dark to light, from glossy to dull. Add the nuts. Put fudge into prepared pan and press into shape with the flat of your palms.

NUTTY CHOCOLATE MINT FUDGE

If there's a mint lover among your family or friends surprise them with this fudge, with it's great after-dinner mint taste.

1 jar (7 oz.) marshmallow crème
1 1/2 cups sugar
1 can (6 oz.) evaporated milk
1/2 cup (1 stick) butter (no
  substitutes)

butter 1/4 tsp. salt
1 1/2 cups mint-chocolate chips
1/2 cup chopped nuts
1 tsp. vanilla

Line an 8-inch square pan with foil. In a heavy saucepan, combine marshmallow crème, sugar, evaporated milk, butter and salt. Bring to a rolling boil over medium heat, stirring constantly. Remove from heat. Add mint chocolate chips and stir until chips are melted and mixture is smooth. Add nuts and vanilla. Pour into prepared pan. Refrigerate until firm.

DORCHESTER FUDGE

Makes about 36 pieces

Try adding 2 teaspoons of instant coffee powder to the sugar-milk mixture for mocha fudge.

1 pkg. (8 oz.) semisweet chocolate
   chips
1/2 cup marshmallow crème
4 tbs. (1/2 stick) butter or margarine,
   softened

1/2 cup chopped walnuts
1/2 tsp. vanilla extract
1 1/2 cups sugar
1 can (6 oz.) evaporated milk

Line an 8-inch square pan with foil. Place chocolate, marshmallow crème, butter, walnuts and vanilla in a bowl; mix and set aside. Combine sugar and evaporated milk in a 2-quart saucepan; cook, stirring constantly, over medium heat until mixture comes to a rolling boil. Boil for 5 minutes, stirring constantly. Carefully pour boiling sugar-milk mixture over chocolate mixture and stir until chocolate is melted. Pour into prepared pan. Refrigerate until firm.

FRONTIER FUDGE

Makes about 90 pieces

The different chocolates in this make it a wonder to try!

1/2 cup (1 stick) butter
1 can (12 oz.) evaporated milk
4 cups sugar
1 pkg. (10 oz.) large marshmallows
2 squares (1 oz. each) unsweetened chocolate, chopped

1 pkg. (12 oz.) semisweet chocolate chips
1 pkg. (12 oz.) milk chocolate chips
1 tbs. vanilla extract
2 cups chopped walnuts or pecans

Line a 9 x 13-inch pan with foil. In a 4- to 6-quart heavy saucepan cook butter, evaporated milk and sugar over medium-high heat until sugar is dissolved and mixture is boiling. Reduce heat to low, cover and continue to boil for 5 minutes without stirring. Remove from heat and stir in marshmallows until melted. Add semisweet chocolate and stir until melted; repeat with milk chocolate. Stir in vanilla and nuts. Pour into prepared pan. Refrigerate until firm.

POTATO FUDGE

Your friends won't believe that you made fudge with mashed potatoes.

3 squares (1 oz. each) unsweetened
  chocolate
3 tbs. butter or margarine
1/3 cup unseasoned mashed
  potatoes
1 tsp. vanilla extract

1 pinch salt
1 lb. confectioner's sugar
1 1/2 tsp. milk, or more if needed
flaked coconut and/or chopped
  walnuts, for garnish

Melt chocolate squares and butter in a saucepan over low heat, stirring constantly. When melted, remove from heat and add mashed potatoes, vanilla and salt. Mix well. Sift confectioner's sugar into a large bowl. Add chocolate mixture, mixing well. Mixture will be crumbly. Add milk as necessary to make a mixture that can be kneaded easily. Turn out on board and knead until smooth. Shape mixture into two logs, each 12 inches long and 1 1/4- inch in diameter. Roll each log into coconut or walnuts. Cut into 1/2-inch thick slices.

HEALTHFUL FUDGE

Makes about 36 pieces

This guilt-free recipe is as yummy as it is nutritious.

1 cup honey
1/2 cup peanut butter
1 cup carob powder
1 cup shelled sunflower seeds
1/2 cup flaked coconut
1/2 cup raisins
1/2 cup toasted sesame seeds
1/2 cup chopped walnuts

Line an 8-inch square pan with foil. In a large saucepan over low heat, melt honey and peanut butter, stirring constantly, just until smooth. Remove from heat. Stir in carob powder; mix well. Add sunflower seeds, coconut, raisins, sesame seeds and walnuts. Press into prepared pan. Refrigerate until firm. Store in refrigerator.

OTHER FUDGES

KAHLÚA FUDGE

This mocha fudge recipe is for adults only!

1 lb. confectioner's sugar
1 cup unsweetened cocoa powder
1/3 cup milk
1/2 cup (1 stick) butter
1/2 cup chopped walnuts
1 1/2 cups marshmallows
3 tbs. Kahlúa liqueur
1 tsp. vanilla extract

Line an 8-inch square pan with foil. Combine sugar, cocoa, milk and butter in a microwave-safe bowl. Microwave on high for 2 minutes. Stir well to blend, then add nuts, marshmallows, Kahlúa and vanilla. Stir until smooth. Pour into prepared pan. Refrigerate until firm.

INDEX